Guidance

WHAT THE BIBLE SAYS ABOUT KNOWING GOD'S WILL

Oliver R. Barclay

*INTER-VARSITY PRESS
DOWNERS GROVE
ILLINOIS 60515*

© Inter-Varsity Press, Leicester, England.
First American printing, October 1978,
by InterVarsity Press,
Downers Grove, Illinois with permission from
Universities and Colleges Christian
Fellowship, Leicester, England.

All rights reserved.
No part of this book may be reproduced in any
form without written permission
from InterVarsity Press, Downers Grove, Illinois.

InterVarsity Press is the book-publishing division
of Inter-Varsity Christian Fellowship,
a student movement active on campus at hundreds of
universities, colleges and schools of nursing.
For information about local and
regional activities, write IVCF, 233 Langdon St.,
Madison, WI 53703.

Distributed in Canada through InterVarsity Press,
1875 Leslie St., Unit 10, Don Mills,
Ontario M3B 2M5, Canada.

Quotations from the Bible are from
the Revised Standard Version, copyrighted 1946 and 1952,
Second Edition 1971, by the Division
of Christian Education, National Council
of the Churches of Christ in the U.S.A.

ISNB 0-87784-304-X

Printed in the United States of America

1	GOD'S PROMISE TO GUIDE	9
2	HOW GOD GUIDES	12
3	BIBLICAL DIRECTION	15
4	WISDOM AND COMMON SENSE	19
5	MAKING UP YOUR MIND	23
6	THE ADVICE OF EXPERIENCE	27
7	SEEKING AFTER SIGNS	30
8	MAKING SENSE OF FEELINGS	33
9	THE ROLE OF CIRCUMSTANCES	42
10	CONDITIONS OF GUIDANCE	47
11	VOCATION, JOB, SERVICE	52
12	AMBITIOUS: TO BE AND NOT TO BE	55

INTRODUCTION

The question of divine guidance can be considered in a number of ways. We can approach it, for example, from the standpoint of experience and examine the ways in which Christians profess to have been guided in the past. Alternately we may consider the subject from a theological or a devotional point of view. The resulting conclusions may then be welded into some sort of system. None of these methods, however, is attempted in this pamphlet, which could best be described as a Bible study on guidance.

My intent is that each chapter should deal with a major aspect of the matter as it is treated in the Bible. These biblical principles are then related to one another without any attempt to create a rigid system to be applied always in every situation. I believe that I have dealt with all the main points emphasized by the Bible. I also believe that the only safe way of obtaining guidance is to adhere strictly to the biblical principles. We must be extremely wary of any other type of guidance, however much it may appear to be sanctified by the experiences of godly men and women in the past.

I
GOD'S PROMISE TO GUIDE

Christians have rarely been in doubt as to *the fact* of divine guidance. In the first place there are numerous assurances throughout the Bible that God will look after his own children. God reveals himself as the Shepherd to his flock and the Father to his children. He delights to turn apparent calamity into blessing. Though the path by which he leads his people is often very hard and unpleasant, he leads them this way only to bring them in the right spirit to the promised land.

At all stages of the history of Israel, as recorded in the Old Testament, and equally in the New Testament, this confidence upheld his children and made them bold to face life and its perplexities, anxious to do what was right. Indeed, the problem of guidance as we know it seems rarely to have arisen, or at least rarely to have been prominent, because the men and women of God were preoccupied with obedience to God. Beyond that they were able to trust their Lord to overrule. "Trust in the LORD and do good; so you will dwell in the land, and enjoy security. Take delight in the LORD, and he will give you the desires of your heart. Commit your way to the LORD, trust in him, and he will act" (Ps. 37:3-5).

It is in this same confidence that we are assured that "in everything God works for good with those who love him, who are called according to his purpose" (Rom. 8:28). That God really does overrule everything in the world and that even the wills of ungodly people are in his hands are assurances which must form the background of all our thinking about guidance and which will put our problems in their proper perspective.

In addition, we are given specific promises that the Lord will lead us. As he says to the psalmist, "I will instruct you and teach you the way you should go; I will counsel you with my eye upon you" (Ps. 32:8).

Again, to a repentant and obedient people, he promises in Isaiah 58:11, "the LORD will guide you continually."

Or, once more, we read in Proverbs 3:5-6, "Trust in the LORD with all your heart, and do not rely on your own insight. In all your ways acknowledge him, and he will make straight your paths." (See also Ps. 25:8-9, 12, 14.)

We are not promised guidance far in advance, nor are we assured that we shall always know how God is going to work; but we are promised that, as and when we need to make decisions, God will overrule and guide.

Many Christians get into quite a state of anxiety over difficult decisions. This is often a failure of faith—not so much faith in particular promises as faith in God's providence. After all, God does know our problems, he does know our weaknesses and the incompleteness of our knowledge; he knows how soon a decision must be made; and, above all, he loves us. Is he not the Lord of hosts, the God of all the earth, who "accomplishes all things according to the counsel of his will"? He promises to look after us and he certainly will do so; therefore, "Even though I walk through the valley of the shadow of death, I fear no evil; for thou art with me" (Ps. 23:4).

2
HOW GOD GUIDES

There are many Christians, however, who, while they are in no doubt about the fact of guidance, are paralyzed when confronted by difficult decisions because they have no real idea *how* God guides. This is the main problem confronting us, and here it is particularly important to be sure that we are biblical in our thinking.

Some people point to the five or six major instances of entirely supernatural guidance in the New Testament and suggest that this is the normal method of guidance for the "spiritual" Christian. An angel of the Lord spoke to Philip the evangelist telling him to go down to the desert where he met the Ethiopian eunuch (Acts 8:26). Peter had a vision guiding him to accept the invitation of Cornelius (Acts 10:1-23). The Holy Spirit spoke to the church at Antioch to send out Paul and Barnabas on the first great overseas missionary journey ever undertaken by Christians (Acts 13:1-3), and this was in confirmation of a personal vision given to Paul earlier (Acts 22:17-21). Paul crossed into Europe only after another vision (Acts 16:6-10).

These instances stand as testimony to the fact that God may guide in an altogether supernatural manner and this is no doubt as true today as it was then. If, however, this was intended to be the normal method of guidance for the Christian, why was it so rare and why are we never promised in Scripture such supernatural leading? A wider study of the Acts and the Epistles makes it clear that normally the apostles were guided by ordinary decisions about the situation before them. The second and third missionary journeys were apparently undertaken simply because the converts needed help (Acts 15:36 and 18:23). When Paul wants to explain to the Corinthians why he will spend the spring in Ephesus instead of visiting them, he says it is because "a wide door for effective work has opened to me, and there are many adversaries," that is to say, because he is needed and not because he "felt led" or because of a vision.

Clearly New Testament Christians expected to be guided by "wisdom," by a sound judgment based on a truly Christian sense of values. Therefore they constantly consulted the apostles and the Old Testament Scriptures to discover what the heavenly wisdom dictated as a solution. Indeed it is this kind of guidance alone which is actually promised in the Bible, as I hope to show in the following pages. "Wisdom" or "judgment" is *promised* to us on certain conditions; and although God may, and sometimes does, guide in other ways, he nowhere promises to do so. In the following pages we shall examine the main promises concerning guidance in order to see what they do really offer us.

3
BIBLICAL DIRECTION

"The LORD is my shepherd, I shall not want; he makes me lie down in green pastures. He leads me beside still waters; he restores my soul. He leads me in paths of righteousness for his name's sake" (Ps. 23:1-3).

The last verse of this familiar quotation is often overlooked. "He leads me in paths of *righteousness*." This is always and everywhere true. Guidance that is not in a path of righteousness is not from God. This is why we are constantly exhorted to search and to know the Bible if we want to be guided by God. If we neglect to discover what is God's clearly revealed will or if, knowing it, we rely on other kinds of "guidance," we shall not be in the line of God's leading.

There is an incident in the life of David (1 Sam. 24) which illustrates this most strikingly. David knew that God had rejected Saul the king and that he himself had been anointed to take his place. But Saul tried to kill David and chased him with an armed force into the wilderness. One day, when David and his men were hiding in the recesses of a cave, Saul came and paused to enter the cave alone. Thereupon David's men said in effect: "Clearly this is God's overruling. He has now given you the means of fulfilling his plan—arise and kill him." But David would not, for he said, "The LORD forbid that I should do this thing to my lord, the LORD's anointed." It cost David probably several years of exile, being chased around the wilderness like a bandit. But he felt bound to do what was right although circumstances had seemingly been overruled so miraculously to give him a short cut to fulfilling the Lord's will.

As if that wasn't enough the same thing happened again not long after, and David took Saul's spear and jar of water from beside him as he slept (1 Sam. 26: 5-12). How easily David could have said, as Abishai in effect did, "Circumstantial guidance! Clearly the Lord intends me to use this slightly doubtful method to accomplish his will." But it was David who wrote the twenty-third psalm.

In 2 Timothy 3:16-17, where we are told of the inspiration and purpose of Scripture, we sometimes forget that the uses of Scripture which are mentioned include: "for correction, and for training in *righteousness*, that the man of God may be complete, equipped for every *good work*." It is clear that, in reading the Bible, we ought constantly to seek practical, ethical instruction; and it is often ignorance of the Bible in this sense that is reponsible for wrong choice.

Certain things are explicitly forbidden in Scripture, and in such cases obedience, not guidance, is required. The man or woman who professes to be guided to marry a non-Christian, for instance, is talking nonsense. It is explicitly forbidden again and again in the Old Testament and implicitly, and quite clearly so, on several occasions in the New. Dishonesty, lying, immorality, snobbishness, selfishness and a whole host of other things are so clearly forbidden in the Bible that we cannot possibly claim to be guided to indulge in them, however excellent we hope the final result may be and however strikingly other factors seem to have pointed to such a course of action. But this does not mean that there is a verse in the Bible for every choice. Neither does it mean that an apparently relevant phrase in the Bible (or in a hymn or *Daily Light*) settles the matter. The devil quoted Scripture to Jesus Christ in his temptation and he may quote it to us, though he nearly always distorts its meaning. We must be sure that we have really understood what the passage concerned means and what it really asks of us on the moral level.

Some people constantly look for guidance in the form of a special verse of Scripture being "given to them." We are never promised this, and it has sometimes led to absurd actions. The missionary candidate assigned to Egypt was right to ignore the fact that in his daily Bible reading he constantly met phrases such as "do not go to Egypt" because the *meaning* of the prohibition was the important thing, not the literal sense when taken out of its context.

On the other hand, as we pray and search our Bible for guidance we may well find some ethical truth or commandment of a general nature which exactly fits our case. The speaker, endeavoring to cancel an engagement previously agreed to, was right to agree to go after all when he happened to read Psalm 15 and found: "Who shall dwell on thy holy hill? He ... who swears to his own hurt and does not change." But this was a principle that should have been taken into account beforehand.

Most of our difficult decisions, however, do not concern anything dealt with directly in the Bible. The primary essential in these cases is a truly Christian sense of values, and this we acquire only as our thinking is increasingly molded by the Bible. We are naturally selfish and we are extraordinarily clever in justifying whatever we want to do. Therefore the first step in guidance is to seek to have a right estimate of the situation. We shall often need a truly Christian attitude to money and to reputation, for instance. Many difficult decisions are essentially questions of how much money is right to spend on ourselves or how much attention we should pay to our own reputation or position in society.

"He leads me in paths of righteousness *for his name's sake*," says David, and we must learn to judge what is most for the honor of his name in every situation and to let that be the most important factor. This is not something that comes to us naturally or easily. It is the fruit of a life constantly reproved and corrected by Scripture, and lived in close fellowship with and obedience to God.

4
WISDOM AND COMMON SENSE

"If any of you lacks wisdom, let him ask God who gives to all men generously and without reproaching, and it will be given him. But let him ask in faith, with no doubting" (Jas. 1:5-6).

The context of this passage is a discussion of the difficulties Christians face in a time of oppression or persecution. In these circumstances we are told to pray for wisdom and to believe that we will be given it. During persecution there are many difficult decisions and it is very hard to keep a right attitude to the oppressor or to the present trials (1:9-18); therefore we need special wisdom and must pray for it. Here is an extremely relevant and quite definite promise for us. When we find ourselves in perplexity, we are to ask for wisdom and we are assured that we shall be given it.

But what exactly is this wisdom? Some have called it "sanctified common sense," but this can be most misleading. James 3:13-18 points out that there is an earthly wisdom and a heavenly wisdom, and that the two are often contrary. The heavenly wisdom is seen in a pure and gracious Christian attitude to people and things. It is the faculty that enables us to steer our way through life in a manner consistent with Christian character. What is promised to us, therefore, is the grace to look at things in a Christian way and to discern what we ought to do accordingly. Often this is at variance with what is called common sense. From the point of view of common sense it is nearly always foolish to enter the ministry or to go abroad as a missionary or to turn the other cheek. It is only heavenly wisdom which considers the real needs of people, and it is only a mind molded by the Bible which is able, in adversity, to look beyond this world to see the things that are unseen and eternal (see Jas. 1:2-4, 9-12).

Here, therefore, we are promised that if we come, humbly recognizing our incompetence, and ask in faith, we shall be given the ability to discern what is the right thing to do. This will not come to us in some magical way nor will it relieve us of the duty of careful thought. The promise is that we shall be enabled to look at the problem "Christianly." In choosing a career, for instance, the Christian will have a completely different *standard of values* from the non-Christian, and it is in the matter of our whole scale of values that the divine wisdom is most commonly distinguished from worldly wisdom.

To take the actual examples given in James 3, if we have been wronged or insulted by someone else, common sense often dictates that we should teach them a lesson or clear our own character or expose their real motives. The wisdom that is from above, on the other hand, "is first pure (concerned with what is right, holy and true), then peaceable, gentle, open to reason, full of mercy and good fruits, without uncertainty or insincerity." Such an attitude and way of looking at things is likely to lead to an opposite policy.

In the matter of an unhappy home, for example, Christian wisdom clearly indicates a determination at all costs to learn to live together and love one another more truly, however difficult that may be. By comparison, the world's wisdom will quickly give up and seek in divorce an easier ("common sense") way out.

There is an instructive example in Acts 6. The church was faced with certain administrative difficulties and the problem was solved by seeking out seven men and putting them in charge of the matter. The grounds for such a solution were simply: "It is not *right* that we should give up preaching the word of God to serve tables.... And what they said pleased the whole multitude." Further, the qualifications of these men were to be three (v. 3): they were to be men of good reputation, "full of the Spirit and of wisdom." That is to say, they were to be men who commanded the confidence of all concerned and who had shown a gift for applying a heavenly mind to down-to-earth problems.

Some Christians show this gift more than others, but we are all invited to seek it as a gift from God and to steer our way through life not by irrational hunches but by the application of revealed truth to real situations. It is only in this sense that we can speak of "sanctified common sense." We must use our ordinary faculties to weigh up a situation and to reach a decision; but our whole outlook on life must be *Christian* and not at all "common" before we start work. We are so extraordinarily adept at thinking out reasons to justify whatever we want to do that it is essential that we should make sure that, all along the line, our standards and criteria have been truly scriptural.

5
MAKING UP YOUR MIND

"He leads the humble in what is right, and teaches the humble his way.... Who is the man that fears the LORD? Him will he instruct in the way that he should choose.... My eyes are ever toward the LORD, for he will pluck my feet out of the net" (Ps. 25:9, 12, 15).

In the end we have to *make up our minds*. God's promise is that he will lead us in our decisions if, on our part, we are open to his leading and control. The whole of Psalm 25 should be studied for some of the conditions of guidance. When we have prayerfully sought to judge the matter in the light of heavenly wisdom and searched the Scriptures for principles bearing on the matter to ensure that, as far as we know, we are not being ruled by false motives, then we have to make a decision and keep to it.

Some people spend hours, and even years, going back over decisions they have made in the past, trying to make up their minds whether they were right or not. But we are to ask for wisdom "in faith, with no doubting" and we are promised that we shall know "what is right" or, as the KJV has it, "the meek will he guide in judgment." This going back over the ground is really doubting the truth of God's promises.

Looking back we often feel that our decisions were not based on all the facts we might have known. But God gives us sufficient information for a decision if we seek it where we are told to look. We can trust him to guide us by giving or withholding from us the facts which would affect our choice. The promise is that at the time he will overrule our judgment so that our decisions are in accordance with his will. It is not that in the light of all the facts we know *afterward* that the decision seems right.

There are an enormous number of possible arguments for or against any particular decision. Some depend on a future which at present cannot be foreseen. God alone foresees that future. You could ask for a hunch to settle the matter irrationally, in which case you would probably end up in a state of constant anxiety in case you've guessed wrong. Alternately and more scripturally you can try to weigh all the factors which you *do* understand and can foresee and then make a decision trusting God to overrule your decision.

You may find later that your choice was wrong because you didn't have all the facts (for example, when your health unexpectedly prevents your going abroad), but that does not alter the fact that God overruled your decision in the end and gave you sufficient reasons to stay home and withheld from you any overwhelming reasons against it. He led you in knowing what was the right thing to do.

Some people become seriously worried about guidance in the trivial matters of daily conduct. They feel, for example, that it might be vitally important which way they walk to go to the store. And they are right, of course; it might be. But they go on from that to a state of constant anxiety and concern lest they do the wrong thing. Sometimes they start one way and have a feeling, after praying about it, that they ought to go back and go the other way. But if these promises about wisdom and judgment are true, we have no right to be anxious and worried like this. We should decide which is the shortest route and which involves least traffic hazards (no Christian has a right to waste time or to risk life and limb needlessly), and decide to go that way. If the Lord really wants us to go the other way tomorrow in order to meet someone, we can believe that he will give us a good *reason* for doing so (for instance, I might remember that I need a new notebook and the best stationery store is over there). We must believe in God's promises and in his providence, and then we can go about our daily work, calmly trusting him to guide our decisions. There is no moral right and wrong about these trivial decisions, and they should be settled by the most matter-of-fact considerations. It is wrong only if we are consciously disobedient to a clear duty that we have.

Even after apparently miraculous guidance we have to make a firm decision, as Paul did after the vision of the man from Macedonia (Acts 16:10). Indeed, the normal guidance in the New Testament seems to have been a matter of clear decisions based on evidence (for example, Acts 6:2-5; 11:28, 29; 15:14-22, 25; 16:3; 20:3, 16; 1 Cor. 16:8, 9). Our difficulty today is partly that we hate making up our minds and we always go on hoping for events to push us into one course of action or another. The Lord does not always allow us to see far ahead but we must constantly make decisions and we must learn to do so in a biblical way in small things if we hope to be able to do so in the big ones.

In practice this means that we must often seek relevant facts. If we are thinking of being a deaconess we must try to discover what the work involves. If we are trying to choose a speaker for our fellowship group we may have to go to some trouble to obtain opinions about speakers from those who know them. When we believe we have sufficient facts, we must decide. We shall never have all the facts that are relevant but we can expect to be led in our decisions when we are adequately informed. It is not more spiritual to keep on postponing decisions in order to pray about them in the hope of getting a hunch. Many people, who wonder whether they are being called to foreign missionary service, remain in uncertainty and doubt partly because they have never bothered to discover what the needs and opportunities of the mission field are. If they knew the facts better they could judge whether they were able to meet the needs.

6
THE ADVICE OF EXPERIENCE

"The way of a fool is right in his own eyes but a wise man listens to advice" (Prov. 12:15).

"Listen to advice and accept instruction, that you may gain wisdom for the future" (Prov. 19:20).

The Bible is far from despising the wisdom that comes with experience of life and of God's dealings with people. In fact there is a repeated emphasis on the need for being humble enough to consult others and in particular those with more experience. Rehoboam was typical of youth, and was at fault when he despised the counsel of the older men and followed only the advice of his contemporaries (1 Kings 12). Further, as Proverbs 12:15 reminds us, it is a characteristic of fools to be content with their own opinion while the truly wise will listen to, and therefore must seek out, the wisest advice available.

Many Christians err here. They seem to be unwilling to humble themselves so far as to admit that an older Christian may have a much better grasp of the heavenly wisdom than they do. But there are people who know the Bible better, know human nature better and can judge our gifts and limitations more impartially than we can ourselves. This is not to say that we should be under bondage to obey our elders and superiors. There are real dangers here, and no one else can get guidance for us (see 1 Kings 13). Nevertheless it is doubtful whether anyone should make a major decision in life, such as what career he should follow, without getting the advice of some experienced Christian.

Many young married couples, for instance, confronted with problems in their marriage, are too proud to consult experienced and wise people and have only themselves to blame for prolonged difficulties and even ultimate disaster. It is interesting that Paul, who had refused to follow advice not to go to Jerusalem because he believed it was his duty to go, nevertheless was willing to obey implicitly the advice given by the elders of the church in Jerusalem (Acts 21:17-26), presumably because they knew the situation in the city better than he did, and no question of moral duty was involved.

It was fashionable at one point for students to give up their university courses halfway in order to go out to the mission field. But these same people, as well as other older Christians, would now certainly advise students first to finish their degrees. The enthusiasm and self-sacrifice involved were admirable, but any older person can see that it is better to give twenty-eight years of first-class missionary service than thirty years of second-class usefulness. For, quite apart from the value of having a degree, youthful enthusiasts may need the mental discipline of a strenuous course to help them to be clearer thinkers, better linguists and people who know how to spend their time. And there are many other factors involved which only older people are likely to be able to weigh fully. That is why missionary societies have committees and churches have selection boards for candidates for the ministry; and the decisions of such bodies are not to be treated lightly, though they are certainly not always the voice of God.

7
SEEKING AFTER SIGNS

"Then Gideon said to God, 'If thou wilt deliver Israel by my hand, as thou hast said, behold, I am laying a fleece of wool on the threshing floor; if there is dew on the fleece alone, and it is dry on all the ground, then I shall know that thou wilt deliver Israel by my hand, as thou hast said' " (Judg. 6:36-37).

Gideon's fleece and a number of similar signs in the Old Testament, together with the few visions and supernatural guidances mentioned in the New Testament, have led some people to believe that they have a right to ask God for a sign or to expect some peculiar personal revelation before they make any important decision. But this is a pure assumption. Nowhere are we encouraged to imitate Gideon, and the signs seem to have been given him, first, because he had no Bible to guide him (or very little of it), and second, because he was so *unspiritual* as to need such signs to bolster his faith in the definite promises which God had already given ("as thou hast said").

In the New Testament no such signs are recorded as were from time to time given to people like Gideon in the Old Testament. The supernatural guidances mentioned in the New Testament are almost all in cases where the guidance given was in order to enlarge their understanding of Scripture (Peter and Cornelius) or was contrary to what appeared reasonable (Philip and the eunuch, Paul and Macedonia). They are mostly over issues that were crucial for the future of the church in a way that is probably hardly ever true of decisions today. If they were intended to be a model for us to follow, the fact would surely have been stated, and the Epistles would have contained some evidence on the subject.

Throughout church history there have been people who have justified the most fantastic and even unchristian deeds (and doctrines) on the grounds of some special vision or sign. And today missionary opportunities have sometimes been neglected in defiance of the clearest wisdom; people have refused to go to posts where they are clearly needed, and Christians have indulged in the grossest folly on the grounds that they had no sign to reassure them or that some supposed sign justified an obviously foolish and even unscriptural course of action.

This is not to say that, as a concession to our lack of understanding and lack of ability to discern God's will, he does not sometimes graciously give such guidance. But we are nowhere encouraged to ask for a sign, and we must always test such peculiar experiences by true wisdom. For the devil can give signs also; and, particularly with people who are psychologically unstable, he often does give visions and hunches which lead them into error or foolishness which is used to disgrace the gospel. Indeed it is probably true that in the majority of cases today where people claim guidance by such means, the so-called signs turn out not to have been of divine origin, and in every case they are difficult to interpret.

A New Testament illustration is supplied by Paul's last visit to Jerusalem. The fact that in every place he visited, Paul was warned, sometimes by means of visions and prophecies (Acts 20:22-24; 21:10-12), that "imprisonment and afflictions" awaited him did not deter him from going, in order to fulfill his clear *duty* (at least in part to hand over to the "poor saints in Jerusalem" the money raised for their relief by the churches of Europe). It is also worth noting that his duty overruled the almost universal requests of his friends. If we had been in Paul's place, the requests of our friends and the supernatural warnings (in this case apparently of divine origin) would have overawed most of us into changing our plans; but not so Paul. It is not clear why these signs were given unless it was to prepare Paul and the churches for the apparent catastrophe of his imprisonment and to reassure them, after the event, that it was part of God's will. In any case they were evidently not to be interpreted as guidance that he should alter his plan.

8
MAKING SENSE OF FEELINGS

"Was I vacillating when I wanted to do this? Do I make my plans like a worldly man, ready to say Yes and No at once?" (2 Cor. 1:17).

In spite of all that has been said, however, it may be argued that surely the Lord will give an inward feeling that we are doing right and, if we have that, it should not be necessary to bother about these other means of guidance. The first answer is that although the Lord often does give such feelings, he nowhere in the Bible promises them, and he often asks his children to act, even in important matters, without them. Second, such inward assurances are notoriously misleading especially when the problem involves something which we very much want to do. Third, even when they lead us in the right direction, such feelings are usually changeable and to some extent at the mercy of our health. Most people become depressed and introspective when they are tired, but quickly recover with some good food and extra sleep. There are people whose feelings are so unstable that they indicate constant changes of direction. To such people one can only say that there is no clearer evidence that their feelings must be ignored. We are to find our "joy and peace in believing," not in feeling.

The apostles showed this independence of feelings by constantly planning ahead. They "purposed" to do something and set about it while recognizing at the same time that God might order things so that their purposes could not be fulfilled (for example, 1 Cor. 16:8, 9; 2 Cor. 1:15-24; Acts 15:36; 16:6-10). In 2 Corinthians 1 Paul is chiefly arguing to defend himself against a charge of changeableness which he agrees would be quite unfitting for a Christian. His reply is that he had powerful reasons for altering his plans. New facts had come to light; the situation had been drastically altered and in the light of the new facts he could no longer fulfill the original purpose of a visit. He gives good sound reasons for his action. He never says that he "felt led." And yet some people say that it is unspiritual to plan ahead!

This is not to say that feelings can be entirely ignored. When we feel unhappy about a course of action it must lead us to think it through again and to make sure that we are not doing wrong. For it is most often when matters of right and wrong are concerned that feelings come in. A business dealing that is not actually dishonest may leave us feeling so uncomfortable that we re-examine it carefully and decide that, although it is not illegal or dishonest, it is at the same time not one hundred per cent honorable. We had perhaps justified our proposed course by careful rationalizations, but our feelings warned us of the need for a decision on a more subtle level. When one path is really known to be right and the other wrong, there is often a real confirmation of our decision by the new peace and joy that come when we decide to do what is right.

But often we find that the matter is not as simple as that. Our feelings are related not only to our conscience but also to our deepest instincts and to our state of health. We may well have little peace of mind about either of the possible alternatives before us, or when we are perfectly willing to do whatever God directs, we may still have no assurance in feeling about anything and be left to make decisions and to follow them out in cold blood.

To take an example, parents should not enjoy punishing their children, and they may find it a profoundly upsetting experience on an emotional level. But it is nonetheless necessary and right at times. Ministers should not enjoy exercising discipline in the church but, because they know it is their duty, they will do it, whatever their feelings may suggest.

Probably many of us have uncomfortable and almost guilty feelings after any strenuous but necessary Christian controversy, and the person who inwardly rejoices in such debate is a menace. But I'm afraid that much **necessary contending for the faith and for righteousness** has been given up prematurely because the resulting strain and disturbed feelings were taken for guidance. Yet in this sinful world we must often force ourselves to do things that are contrary to our natural inclinations and appetites. Those of Christian character are capable of doing extremely distasteful tasks in a straightforward manner.

In the matter of marriage this becomes particularly important. The joy and general sense of well-being that often (but not always) goes with being in love can easily silence conscience and inhibit critical thinking. How often people say that they "feel led" to get married (and probably they will say, "the Lord has so clearly guided") when all they are really describing is a particularly novel state of endocrine balance which makes them feel extremely sanguine and happy. And this comes at a stage when they most need to take counsel from their elders and parents, and to sit down and think as calmly as possible. Subsequent broken engagements and even unhappy homes have shown that they had not adequately considered the basic human problems and qualities involved in marriage. Whatever we may think of Victorian lovers, it is surprising how successful they were in making stable homes. Yet perhaps it is not surprising: for they refused to get engaged until they had seen each other in their own homes, and the necessity of obtaining parental consent forced them to pay an unwonted attention to wisdom and counsel.

Some readers are likely to feel that I have forgotten the work of the Holy Spirit. They do not suggest that inward convictions are a substitute for wisdom and judgment; but according to one tradition of thought, we should not act until there is added to the objective criteria mentioned so far an inward assurance and conviction which the Holy Spirit gives. Romans 8:14, "For all who are led by the Spirit of God are sons of God," is sometimes quoted in this connection. But the context of this verse makes it perfectly clear that what is being demanded is holiness of life, and it is stated that no one should profess to be a son of God who does not show *by his holy living* that he is being led by God.

The whole problem of guidance, after all, is to know *how* the Holy Spirit guides—what means he has chosen to use—and my contention is that he has never promised to lead us by inward convictions but only by wisdom, judgment and advice based upon knowledge of and obedience to the Scriptures.

God does often give an assurance; but usually it is related not so much to an inward feeling as to a growing realization that the proposed course of action is in accordance with true wisdom. Candidates for missionary service are likely to find, as their understanding of the job increases and as they begin to prepare and train for it, all sorts of small evidences that this is indeed their true vocation. If they inspect their feelings, they may well be pursuing a course of violent oscillation between fear of launching out (and perhaps being a failure) and confident assurance in God's power. If they are leaving aged parents or other loved ones their feelings *ought* to be upset by the prospect. But as things proceed they are increasingly assured in their *minds* that this course of action is the right one.

It is worth mentioning here also that the passage in Isaiah 30:20-21 which is often quoted in support of guidance by our inner feelings probably refers in the first place to the promise of wise counselors (KJV and RV have "thy teachers" for "your Teacher"). The passage reads, "And though the LORD give you the bread of adversity and the water of affliction, yet your Teacher will not hide himself any more, but your eyes shall see your Teacher. And your ears shall hear a word behind you, saying, 'This is the way, walk in it,' when you turn to the right or when you turn to the left." It is clear that the "word" which they will hear is the word of "your Teacher," but he will be *visibly* present. That is to say it is a promise that the day will come when the people of God will not be left without a reliable teacher whom they will see and hear amongst them. He will faithfully warn them when they sin and cause them to repent and so deliver them from God's judgments (vv. 22-26).

There is nothing here about an inward hunch. The use of the capital for "Teacher" is the translator's introduction (in the Hebrew it is not necessarily a title and there are no capitals). But even if "the Teacher" is meant to be the Holy Spirit, it is still a visible, unmistakable messenger whose word we hear. This presumably refers to the fuller revelation of the New Testament given to us in Scripture or to the first Christians in the teachings of Christ and his apostles. There is nothing here to suggest that the Holy Spirit will speak to us in inward hunches and intuition. As Peter puts it in 2 Peter 1:18-21, "we have the prophetic word made more sure" even than the "voice borne from heaven" which they heard with their physical ears on the mount when Jesus was transfigured.

This passage from Isaiah has often been used to suggest that we cannot be guided when stationary and that we must make decisions and go ahead and expect to be checked as and when we go wrong. This is no doubt wise advice, and it is perfectly true that to dither over a decision for too long leads to psychological strain and after a time the inability to make decisions about anything. If what I have said about judgement and wisdom is true, then it is our duty to decide and go ahead until it is made clear that we must change our course. But the correction is likely to come from unexpected circumstances (2 Cor. 1), obviously wrong consequences which we had not foreseen, the advice of friends or a new appreciation of a scriptural truth which we had previously overlooked.

A missionary candidate may be prevented at the last moment from going abroad, for instance, by her mother's sudden illness or by someone bringing home to her that she is disobeying the instruction to fulfill previous obligations. It is better to make the decision and plan to go, if that seems right, and then realize that it just would not be possible, than to hover on the brink of decision too long.

Sometimes the real consequences of a decision are hard to assess until you have started to carry it out. Many Christians have to make important decisions with their feelings in a hopeless turmoil. Often they find no assurance for a long time; but, after they have followed the chosen path for some months or years, it becomes increasingly clear that the Lord did, as he promised, give wisdom.

A woman may, for instance, refuse an offer of marriage from a Christian man for good reasons, but be left with deeply disturbed feelings about her decision for years. Often it is only very much later that it is confirmed beyond any possible doubt that that was the right course. Time may bring overwhelming assurance through good reasons which were not at first appreciated. The same is probably true of most vocations; it is only after a while that it becomes absolutely clear what is right and a change of plans does not necessarily mean that we made a mistake in the first place, as we saw with Paul. It may be that we were intended to start that way and change later on. Like David, we may find that: "Whereas it was in your heart to build a house for my name, you did well that it was in your heart; nevertheless you shall not build the house" (2 Chron. 6:8-9).

When all has been said, however, many Christians have at times had very strong feelings that they ought to go and do something or see someone when they can think of no logical reason for doing so. The biographies of some Christians relate instances of this sort where clearly the inward urge was God's way of guiding. Such guidance must be checked by more objective standards, and it would seem to be our duty to pray that God will rather give us *reasons* for such actions. Certainly there is no indication in the Bible that it is "spiritually minded" to be controlled by such feelings and urges as a matter of general practice. We must, however, agree that God may lead us in this way where the decision is strictly neutral from a moral point of view and no objective guidance is available. Owing to our ignorance and sinful lack of sensitivity to the needs of others, there may be no other way of showing us the path.

9
THE ROLE OF CIRCUMSTANCES

"We know that in everything God works for good with those who love him, who are called according to his purpose" (Rom. 8:28).

It is often stated that guidance can come by way of circumstances, and this is, of course, perfectly true, because God creates and controls circumstances. But such guidance is by no means easy to determine. The devil is apparently allowed, not only to arrange signs, but also to bring about remarkable coincidences to tempt us to evil. We have already mentioned the remarkable circumstantial "guidance" to do wrong which David received. We do not know if he argued from circumstantial guidance when he happened to see Bathsheba bathing; but many people have justified obviously wrong marriages or even divorces because of some exceptional coincidence attendant on their meeting.

Yet circumstances are clearly not irrelevant, as a few biblical examples may show. In the first place, negatively, circumstances may absolutely forbid some course of action. Paul in his missionary journeys seems to have moved on to a new place whenever persecution reached such a pitch that public ministry was no longer possible. Equally, he always preached first in the synagogues; but when they rejected the message, he changed his method and went to the Gentiles.

There was also positive guidance from circumstances. Paul's appeal to Caesar (Acts 25:11) seems to have been finally determined by circumstances because it was the only escape from murder on the way up to Jerusalem or perhaps from an indefinitely prolonged imprisonment. He clearly hoped that this would lead to his being set free. Paul also knew how to seize sudden and unexpected opportunities as at Athens, where he immediately took his chance of speaking on Mars Hill.

At the same time Paul and the other New Testament Christians were not put off by adverse circumstances from an energetic and confident evangelistic ministry. For example, when the rulers began to persecute them, in Acts 4, they did not pray for the persecution to be removed but only that they might have the grace to go on witnessing boldly with signs following (Acts 4:29-30). Circumstances seem to have been accepted as guidance only when they rendered an apparently desirable course of action impossible or morally wrong or else when they opened unexpected opportunities for doing good. This was presumably because of their confidence in God's control of all things in the world.

Probably every Christian has had examples of this kind of thing in his own life. Ill health has prevented attending an interview for a job. Missing a train by mistake has brought profitable conversation with a fellow passenger. In the story of our own conversion there were probably incidents, not all planned by us, but important in bringing us under the sound of the gospel or making us open-minded toward the gospel. We accept these things as part of God's providential control of "all things according to the counsel of his will," and we are grateful for the confidence that so long as we follow what we believe to be right, he can and will overrule our circumstances to keep us from evil and from doing anything damaging to his purposes. We must have this confidence as Christians or we would be driven to distraction by anxiety about our decisions.

This is a further context in which prayer is important. Often we are moved to pray that God will remove some apparently insuperable barrier, and if he does we have the greatest confidence that the plan is a right one. Some missionary societies, for instance, habitually delay new and apparently desirable developments until at least a part of the necessary money is available for the purpose. In this way they test the guidance which they believe they have been given through wisdom. There are obviously limits to this because we have no promise that God will give us a sign; but where it is a matter of circumstances making possible what at first seemed impossible though right, we are not asking a sign in Gideon's sense but only asking God to open the way for us to obey him along this particular path. A young missionary candidate, for example, may be prevented from sailing by the stubborn opposition of parents or a mother's ill health, and she may well pray for these obstacles to be removed.

On the other hand if such prayer is not answered, we must accept the guidance that God gives by making circumstances impossible. Often he has a better plan. At the time of the rise of Communism in China many people prayed, and prayed believingly, that freedom for missionary work would not be lost. This prayer was not answered positively and the triumph of Communism seemed to be a disaster. Now, however, some years afterward, we can see a little part of the reason. Hundreds of missionaries have been released for work in other and in some cases even less evangelized areas, and it seems that this was part of the reason why history was allowed to take this course. Paul spent most, if not all, of his stay in Rome as a prisoner. This was clearly not the way in which he expected to arrive or to minister there; but it is doubtful whether he could have lived and ministered for so long unmolested by the Jews if he had been free to go as he pleased through the city.

Nevertheless it must be repeated that no Christian should wait to be pushed around by his circumstances. Life is not intended to be a bed of roses and there are many times when wisdom or direct duty require that we adopt a seemingly foolish or almost impossible course of action, and those of Christian faith and vision will not be deterred. No Christian who weakly sits down under difficulties and murmurs "circumstantial guidance" would be commended by the apostles for his attitude.

10
CONDITIONS OF GUIDANCE

"He leads the humble in what is right.... those who keep his covenant and his testimonies.... the man that fears the LORD" (Ps. 25:9-10, 12).

The promises of guidance are made on certain conditions. This may seem obvious, but it is not always remembered, and some of those who are most perplexed by questions of guidance are perplexed because they are not paying attention to these conditions.

In the first place, only committed Christians are promised any guidance at all. It is "with those who love him" that "in everything God works for good." Guidance may at times be given to others in order to lead them to repentance and faith, but only those who are true Christians have a right to turn to God in prayer and claim his help and favor in perplexity.

Second, we must say that sincere obedience to God is a condition of guidance. "If I had cherished iniquity in my heart, the LORD would not have listened" (Ps. 66:18). If there is deliberate disobedience in our lives or in our attitudes, we cannot expect his fatherly and gracious leading, but only his correction and chastising. One hears of Christians who are absorbed in some difficult and apparently insoluble problem of guidance whose real problem turns out to be a matter of *known* sin in their life. The question of guidance seems to have been merely a distraction to enable the mind to forget the real issue.

Psalm 25, however, and many similar passages lay their stress not so much on deliberate sin as on a wrong attitude. They insist on the need for an attitude of meekness, teachableness and humility. "God," we are warned, "opposes the proud, but gives grace to the humble" (1 Pet. 5:5). It is a mockery to ask for wisdom if we are not willing and eager to obey God's will once it is discerned. Some people ask for guidance with regard to a career but refuse to go to missionary meetings in case they should receive a call to the mission field. In Psalm 32, after promising to guide us, God adds, "Be not like a horse or a mule, without understanding, which must be curbed with bit and bridle, else it will not keep with you." That is to say, if we want guidance we must be willing to obey intelligently. It should be the desire of every Christian at all costs to obey God and to please him. As soon as we depart from this attitude, we are likely to be in difficulties.

Probably every Christian has at times had difficulty here. Particularly in decisions that concern something we very much want to do, it is hard to be sure that we are not merely indulging in wishful thinking or asking God to confirm a course of action that we have already determined. If we are honest we shall never be certain that our motives are absolutely pure. We know our own hearts too well. In such a decision we must pray for a true objectivity and ask God to give us such an overriding desire for his honor and glory that we are able to judge aright. But it is no good indulging in endlesss introspection. We must make allowance for our own selfishness and get on. By all means we must pray about it and ask to be given a willingness which does not come naturally to us and a fresh love for him which makes selfish consideration small. But then we must turn to the objective task of seeking out the divine wisdom of the matter, determined that, by God's grace, we will obey whatever is right. And what is right is not always the most unpleasant or the most reckless alternative.

It is here that the day-by-day devotional life of the Christian comes in. If we are not abiding in Christ our standard of values can quickly become debased. And if we are not making full use of the means of grace at our disposal, our devotional life is not likely to remain sincere and fresh for long. We may, of course, retain all the pious shibboleths, but they can easily become a mere habit of speech. We must see to it that our *affections* as well as our intellect are set on pleasing God. Or, to put it in terms of Psalm 25, "For thee I wait all the day long.

... The friendship of the LORD is for those who fear him. ... My eyes are ever toward the LORD; for he will pluck my feet out of the net." Or as James puts it on the negative side, "You ask and do not receive, because you ask wrongly, to spend it on your passions" (Jas. 4:3).

Third, we may say that prayer is a condition of guidance. "If any of you lacks wisdom, let him ask God" (Jas. 1:5). It is easier than it sounds to neglect this and to become so preoccupied with thinking out the problem that we forget to pray. At the same time we must remember that we are not heard for our excessive talk. To spend an hour worrying on our knees is not prayer.

Indeed, there are often times when it is our duty, having committed a problem to God in prayer, to stop praying, to trust and to do the necessary work to arrive at a solution. If a problem becomes worrisome, this is probably always the case. It may then be helpful to talk to someone and perhaps pray with him or her about it; but few, if any of us are able in solitary prayer to do more than worry on our knees after a short time. The longer we spend and the more tired we become, the more impossible it is to give ourselves to intercession on the matter. We simply let our difficulty go round and round in our minds.

The place of prayer is more usually that we should mention our need before God repeatedly. Let it be something placed daily in his wise, loving and holy hands and left there with confidence. Many Christians, a long time before marriage can be reasonably contemplated, pray about the matter; and it is good also, as soon as our decisions begin to seriously affect our future, to pray that we may be led aright in the matter of our vocation. Then, when these become pressing problems requiring decision, we can the more easily trust God and pray believingly for his wisdom.

These conditions are simple but basic. They concern our daily walk with Christ and are matters which are in any case our Christian duty and privilege quite apart from any particular needs. It should not require crises in our lives to persuade us of their necessity or to show us that they have been neglected.

II
VOCATION, JOB, SERVICE

"Doing the will of God from the heart" (Eph. 6:6).

When the Bible deals with the matter of doing God's will, it is less concerned with the problems of discovering it than with the difficulty of doing it. I have focused on discovering it, but many of the problems of guidance arise from a failure to think about "ordinary" work in the way that the Bible does, to see that the Christian's vocation could as readily be to scrub floors as to preach. Not everyone is meant to preach, and to most of us an "ordinary" job is not a second best.

In this passage in Ephesians 6 Paul is urging both slaves and masters to do their work in such a way that they see it as doing the will of God. Only in this way can it be done "from the heart," wholeheartedly, especially when, as slaves, it was often exceedingly unpleasant. It must be possible to see our job or our other roles in society in this same way today. Indeed we *must* do so. We must work toward an attitude that makes our tasks a vocation from God.

The difficulty arises from a failure to take in two truths that are implied in this passage. First, there is the fact that in carrying out our tasks we are pleasing and serving God. That, he says, is true even of tasks we didn't choose to do ourselves. As it says in the next verse (Eph. 6:7), "rendering service with a good will as to the Lord and not to men." That is to say we do this job for him because *he* wants it done. So we do it with a good will. How can we do less if he cares about it and if it matters to him how the task is carried out?

But that is not all. Slaves' work is rightly translated here as "service." Jesus reminded us that our heavenly Father makes "his sun rise on the evil and on the good, and sends rain on the just and on the unjust" (Mt. 5:45) and went on to tell us to be like him in that attitude. Therefore any task that can be said to be helpful to anyone else (even to a cruel slave master) is doubly satisfactory. But most jobs fall into that category. They may only do so indirectly by increasing employment or wealth, improving education or health, or advancing people's knowledge and understanding of God's world and of human nature.

The Christian, therefore, should be capable of enthusiasm for most jobs on both counts, and this in not the only New Testament passage where this positive enthusiasm for plain manual or other "secular" work is required of Christians. He is expected to have a real sense of vocation in his work. Even if it is not the job we would have chosen and has no directly spiritual components, it is our task to give it that spiritual dimension.

This traditional biblical doctrine of vocation has been sadly neglected recently. Indeed in some circles a vocation means a call to the full-time ministry of the church. But that is far from the New Testament idea. If slaves' work could take on this important character, how much more easily should work in industry, business, teaching and a hundred and one other jobs that do not involve the direct ministry of the Word? In some we have to think hard about their positive value to society but, with few exceptions, they are a part of God's task for us in his world and, therefore, worthy vocations.

In others (for example, medicine and social work) we easily lose the divine perspective because the service aspect is so clear. But we must think our way through to a position where we rejoice in a role as a vocation in which we can serve God and people. The Bible shows that a truly Christian mind will see the most menial jobs in this light. Much frustration and disappointment with our present job is saved if we learn to see it like this, even while we may be looking for something more suited to our training and ability.

12
AMBITIOUS: TO BE AND NOT TO BE

"Whoever would save his life will lose it, and whoever loses his life for my sake will find it" (Mt. 16:25).

"Seek first his kingdom and his righteousness, and all these things shall be yours as well" (Mt. 6:33).

There is, according to these sayings, a certain perversity built into life. Those who energetically seek their own good, will fail to find it, while those who have their aims set on God's purposes rather than their own, will find that their needs are met. Indeed, we find ourselves by looking outside ourselves. Real life is given where life is surrendered.

The first question we need to ask therefore is not how a decision may affect me and my little world (God is looking after that), but rather we need to ask what God's purposes are and how they are best fulfilled. These may be purposes which have little to do with my desires. Nevertheless God promises that those who are so orientated will find what they need. We can and should be enthusiastically caught up in the great privilege of serving God even while we gladly shed some superficial ambitions in that pursuit.

A high proportion of the population, for instance, complains about lack of job satisfaction. The main reason for that seems to be simply that they are trying to *find* job satisfaction. The more they chase that ideal, the more elusive it becomes. Meanwhile, one of the marks of a Christian is that he has an enthusiasm for his job. That is not because it provides a satisfying end in itself but precisely because he sees and aims beyond it. In that wider aim he finds satisfaction in his job (Col. 3:22-24).

Many non-Christians say that they find marriage and the home restricting and stuffy. But what can they expect if they thought that marriage in itself would be totally satisfying? This marvelous gift of God is a very inadequate God-substitute. If we try to make it our idol, we find it most disappointing. And yet, working together for the glory of God, it is one of the greatest gifts given to us. A marriage directed like that is enriched tremendously and provides much of what people look for when they try to make it an end in itself.

This is not to suggest that the job, the home, the career, are simply means to an end (see chapter eleven). Christians must be concerned to glorify God in the way that they live and act in every area of their lives. As a result they enjoy them more than the man or woman to whom success is everything.

At the same time the Bible does encourage a certain kind of ambition. Indeed, it demands it of us. Paul, in Philippians 1, puts it like this, "To me to live is Christ, and to die is gain.... I am hard pressed between the two. My desire is to depart and be with Christ, for that is far better. But to remain in the flesh is more necessary on your account. Convinced of this, I know that I shall remain and continue with you all..." (vv. 21, 23-25).

This gives us a remarkable glimpse of his inner priorities. Of course, he would love to be with Christ, finally freed from sin, enjoying unhindered worship of heaven. But even that is not his priority. It is more important to him to be useful to the church and to the spread of the gospel. His concern is to complete the job given to him and to serve people while he can. He puts that before his own spiritual blessedness.

So we are to be ambitious! We are to seek God's kingdom with all our energies. That does not only mean to seek the spread of the gospel. It means a concern for all that furthers his will for everyone. We are also to be concerned to be useful to others while we can. Even though Paul is speaking in the context of Christian ministry, the same rule applies in due proportion to other roles in life. There is a necessary Christian ambition to develop our gifts and then to use them for the very best—to be as useful as possible.

Let us suppose that there are three teaching posts advertised in the paper for all of which you are professionally qualified: high-school principal, high-school math teacher and school counselor. If you want one of these jobs you should first try to judge your gifts, then you can decide what fits in with your own long-term ambitions of Christian usefulness. Being principal has the prestige and the money (and the long hours); the mathematics job demands real skill as a teacher and love of the subject; the counselor's job requires primarily pastoral gifts. It is doubtful whether you should apply for any of these jobs unless you have reason to think that you can do them well or can *grow* into doing them well. For instance the good classroom teacher is not always a good administrator or a good counselor. On the other hand your accumulated experience may well equip you to take the more prestigious job of principal and to stretch your capacity to give to the community in that way. Your influence in the community will be greater though less personal if you are the principal. If, however, your real gift is pastoral, at least at this stage in your life, you will be frustrated as principal and will probably do it badly. But if you can separate your personal ambition for the boosting of your ego from your duty to do your utmost to serve God and people, then you should be ambitious.

Baruch was told by Jeremiah, "Do you seek great things for yourself? Seek them not" (Jer. 45:5). That is a word we all have to take to heart. But the crucial point is the phrase "for yourself." At the same time we are told to be "zealous for good deeds" (Tit. 2:14), a phrase which could be paraphrased "be ambitious to do good." It is easy to settle down and accept the mediocre, a way of life which is free from doing harm but which does not use our capacities for the glory of God or for the community. This Christian ambition may lead us to some decisions that surprise others. We may opt for teaching in a tough and unpopular area. We may not want the top job. On the other hand it rightly leads some Christians to push to the top and to compete for posts which develop their abilities in areas that the community or the profession badly needs. We are not meant always to be feverishly active, but we are told to "be steadfast, immovable, always abounding in the work of the Lord, knowing that in the Lord your labor is not in vain" (1 Cor. 15:58).

further reading from InterVarsity Press

The Fight: A Practical Handbook for Christian Living
John White offers refreshing insights to guidance and other basic areas of the Christian life—including prayer, Bible study, evangelism, faith, fellowship and work. paper, $3.95

Grow Your Christian Life
Personal daily Bible study on topics such as knowing God's will, personal evangelism, sin and Christian marriage. paper, $2.50

Basic Christianity
John Stott presents a clear statement of the fundamental content of Christianity and urges the non-Christian to consider the claims of Christ. paper, $1.50

Affirming the Will of God
Paul Little discusses the prerequisites for knowing the will of God, the principles for following the will of God and the common mistakes that Christians make in regard to both. paper, 25¢

The Cost of Commitment
John White explains that following God's will often involves great cost as he discusses obedience and what it means to suffer for Jesus' sake. paper, $1.95

Daring to Draw Near
John White examines the prayers of David, Job, Daniel, Christ and five other people in the Bible who look to God for answers and strength, seeking to follow him and his will. paper, $3.95

Knowing God
J. I. Packer discloses the nature and character of God and how to get to know him, not only informing the mind but warming the heart and inspiring devotion. cloth, $5.95; paper, $3.95

Everything You Want to Know about the Mission Field, but Are Afraid You Won't Learn until You Get There
Charles Troutman's letters reveal what to expect from the local church, the surrounding culture and the mission board for those seeking God's will about going overseas. paper, $2.95